Count It All Joy

31 Days of Faith and Gratitude

JOY PITTMAN

Table of Contents

Introduction

You know as well as I do that life can sometimes feel like a rollercoaster. It can have some very high peaks and some pretty low valleys. But here's a reminder hidden deep in the core of our faith; we can find an undeniable, unshakeable joy. It's there, even when things seem out of alignment and off balance.

This 31-day journey we're about to step into is about finding that joy. It's not about bypassing the hard stuff. Rather it's about building our faith on the fact that a loving and gracious God has us in mind - even in the midst of our trials. We'll get real, delve into Scriptures, share some heartfelt prayers, and maybe even unpack parts of our lives that we've kept neatly tucked away.

Each day, we will build on the foundation of faith and joy provided to us in James 1: 2-4, using it as our blueprint. Some days will be about savoring the joy in serving God, others about understanding the depth of faith grounded in God's character. And yes, we'll also talk about obedience, the rewards of keeping faith, and the outcomes of straying away.

As we walk this path together, consider this devotional your daily dose of spiritual nourishment, a place to reconnect with the joy that is INHERENTLY OURS as children of God.

So, ready or not - here we go! I'm right here with you, excited to walk this journey alongside you, cheering you on every step of the way.

I love you and I am excited that we get to "Count It All Joy" together!

-Joy

PRAYER

Loving Father, as we embark on this 31-day journey, we first pause to acknowledge Your sovereignty and grace that has led us to this transformative moment. Your word says in Philippians 4:13, "I can do all things through Christ who strengthens me." We lean into that promise now, asking for Your divine strength and guidance throughout this devotional journey.

God, for every reader, for every soul that is about to dive into these pages, I pray that You provide a tenacious spirit, one that is determined to finish this course and emerge stronger, more joy-filled, and deeply rooted in You. As the days unfold and life's demands knock on our doors, remind us, O Lord, to prioritize this time with You, drawing from the well of Your wisdom and peace.

May Your Spirit illuminate every word, making it resonate within our hearts. Encourage us, Lord, when the journey seems long, and grant us the perseverance to press on, knowing that with every day, we are drawing closer to a deeper connection with You.

Strengthen our resolve, renew our spirits daily, and may this devotional experience be one that etches Your truths deep within us, setting the tone for all our days to come.

In the strong name of Jesus, we pray. Amen.

DAY 1

Embracing Joy in Trials

Scripture Focus:

"Consider it pure joy, my brothers and sisters, whenever you face trials of many kinds, because you know that the testing of your faith produces perseverance. Let perseverance finish its work so you may be mature and complete, not lacking anything." (James 1:2-4, NIV)

Let's Get Into It:

Sometimes life can be hard. The things we encounter can seem unfair and it can feel like God doesn't see what we are going through or care about how bad it feels. BUT the truth is he absolutely sees and cares. In this scripture, James encourages us to see the hard moments through a different perspective. He basically tells us to get out of our feelings and dig into our faith - and then he takes it a step further and tells us to "count it all joy"

1

Now I am clear how unrealistic or even absurd it sounds to associate joy with trials. But James tells us to look past the experience and see what the experience is revealing to us. James reminds us that joy is not dependent on external circumstances, but it stems from the understanding that trials are an avenue for personal and spiritual growth. Our faith is refined and matured as we persevere, leading us to a state of completeness, "not lacking anything." It's like gold refined through fire, emerging purer and more precious (1 Peter 1:6-7).

Let's look at the story of Job as an example (Job 1:21). While it appeared to everyone, including his friends that his trials were some negative results of something he had done - the story tells us that it was because of God considering him. AND while Job was a good and upright man already we can see him being matured and made even more complete through his suffering - to the extent that he is able to find compassion and pray for the healing of his friends.

Our faith in God is not just in his ability. We also have to trust his intentions. We must know that even the hard moments are working in our favor and designed to make us better.

Let Us Pray:

"Gracious and Loving Father, thank you for seeing me, being mindful of me, and always ready to help me. Today, I

ask that you help me find joy in the midst of trials, relying on Your guidance and building my faith in who you are.

Help me to trust You more deeply, to be able to find peace in Your presence even when I am faced with challenges. Lord, as I navigate through this day, let me lean on Your promises and Your strength, finding joy in Your enduring love and grace.

I pray with a trusting heart; I commit this day into Your hands. I trust that You will lead me in paths of righteousness.

I thank you in advance for the manifestation of Your love and grace. And I count these things as done in the strong name of Jesus. Amen."

Now, as you continue through your day, find moments to re-empower yourself. Take a moment to reflect on this scripture and reflection:

- Psalm 28:7, "The Lord is my strength and my shield; my heart trusts in him, and he helps me. My heart leaps for joy, and with my song I praise him." (NIV).

- I trust God's ability AND His intentions towards me. I know He has by best interest at heart and will work everything out for my good.

Joy Pittman

DAY 2

Faith that Transforms

Scripture Focus:

"Do not conform to the pattern of this world, but be transformed by the renewing of your mind. Then you will be able to test and approve what God's will is — his good, pleasing and perfect will." (Romans 12:2, NIV)

Let's Get Into It:

In a world full of so many different and sometimes conflicting ideas, it's easy to just go with what everyone else seems to be thinking. But the verse Romans 12:2 nudges us to think differently, to let our faith freshly shape our minds. Here, faith isn't just about what we believe in, it's a powerful force that can change how we see things, bringing us closer to God's loving perspective.

Sometimes, being a believer means having a way of thinking that doesn't get caught up in the day-to-day

5

stuff but is instead renewed time and again through a close bond with God. This kind of faith helps us understand God's kind, loving, and perfect plans, even when things get really complicated. A perfect example of this is how the Apostle Paul changed. He went from hunting down Christians to becoming one of the most devoted followers (Acts 9:1-19). Paul's story shows us how deep and changing a real connection with God can be.

Let Us Pray:

"Dear Heavenly Father, thank you for Your eternal wisdom and the perfect design You have for my life. Today, I am reminded of Your call in Philippians 4:8 to focus on whatever is true, noble, right, and pure. I come before You, seeking the grace to cultivate a mind that aligns with these divine standards.

I ask for Your guidance in nurturing a transformative faith, and reshaping my perspective to mirror Your goodness and grace. Lead me, Lord, in thought and action, so that I may embody the virtues You hold dear, displaying a life that is pleasing and perfect in Your sight.

Lord, I trust that You are guiding my steps, helping me to think and act in ways that bring glory to Your name. I place my faith in Your sovereign hand, trusting that You are fashioning a future filled with hope.

In the strong name of Jesus, I pray. Amen."

As you continue through your day, find moments to re-empower yourself. Here are some prompts you can reflect and meditate on:

- Philippians 4:8, "Finally, brothers and sisters, whatever is true, whatever is noble, whatever is right, whatever is pure, whatever is lovely, whatever is admirable — if anything is excellent or praiseworthy — think about such things." (NIV).

- Ask God to guide you in fostering a transformative faith that reshapes your perspective and aligns your thoughts and actions with His good, pleasing, and perfect will.

Joy Pittman

DAY 3

The Joy of Service

Scripture Focus:

"You, my brothers and sisters, were called to be free. But do not use your freedom to indulge the flesh; rather, serve one another humbly in love." (Galatians 5:13, NIV)

Let's Get Into It:

As we navigate through our spiritual journey, it becomes apparent that our faith isn't just a personal haven but a gateway to impacting the lives around us. One of the most profound expressions of our faith and love is serving others selflessly. Galatians 5:13 beckons us to utilize our freedom in Christ as a platform to serve one another humbly in love, steering clear from the indulgences of the flesh.

Embracing a servant's heart doesn't demean or diminish us; instead, it amplifies the character of Christ within us. Just as Jesus exemplified through His life —

washing His disciples' feet as a sign of humility and service (John 13:14-17) — we, too, are called to find joy and fulfillment in serving others. Through these selfless acts, we embody Christ's love, fostering unity and harmony within our communities.

Let Us Pray:

"Gracious God, I stand before You, assured that You notice and remember each act of love and kindness I extend to Your people. Today, I am fueled by the comforting promise that You do not overlook our actions and efforts in serving you and others. I rely heavily on Your guidance, trusting that You are molding me into a reflection of Your grace and compassion in this world.

Lord, I ask for Your guidance to nurture within me a heart eager to serve others with a pure motive. Shape me into a vessel of Your endless love, ready to channel blessings and joy to those around me. In the mighty name of Jesus, I pray. Amen."

As you continue through your day, find moments to re-empower yourself. Here are some prompts you can reflect and meditate on:

- Hebrews 6:10, "God is not unjust; he will not forget your work and the love you have shown him as you have helped his people and continue to help them." (NIV).

- Seek God's guidance to mold you into someone eager to serve others with love and joy, creating ripple effects of His love in your surroundings.

Joy Pittman

DAY 4

Obedience in Faith

Scripture Focus:

"If you love me, keep my commands." (John 14:15, NIV)

Let's Get Into It:

Obedience is a term that sometimes carries a burden of grudging submission or loss of autonomy. However, in the spiritual context, obedience blossoms from a place of love and a deep-rooted faith. As we delve into John 14:15, we encounter a profound truth: obeying God is a true testament to our love and faith in Him.

Through obeying God's commands, we foster an enriched relationship with Him, echoing the harmonious rapport between Jesus and His Father throughout the scriptures. The Bible is replete with narratives showcasing the blessings and favor that accompany obedience. A compelling example can be seen in Abraham, who was commended for his faith and obedience when he was willing to sacrifice his son Isaac at God's command (Genesis 22:1-18).

Let Us Pray:

"Dear Heavenly Father, thank you for your clear guidance found in your word, reminding us of the essence of true worship and devotion to you. Your instructions illuminate the path of righteousness, guiding us in the way we should go.

Today, I humbly ask for your grace to embrace obedience wholeheartedly in my daily walk with you. Lord, cultivate within me a heart that desires to comply with your commands, not out of obligation, but out of genuine love and reverence for you. Help me to prioritize your will above all else, understanding that obedience to your word brings more honor to you than any sacrifice I could offer.

I pray that each day, my relationship with you deepens, fostering a closer connection characterized by love-fueled compliance with your divine will. I rely on you, Lord, to shape my heart and align my actions with your precepts.

In Jesus' strong name, I pray. Amen."

As you continue through your day, find moments to re-empower yourself. Here are some prompts you can reflect and meditate on:

- 1 Samuel 15:22, "To obey is better than sacrifice, and to heed is better than the fat of rams." (NIV).

- Ask for God's grace to walk daily in obedience, fostering a closer, more genuine relationship with Him, where love fuels every act of compliance.

Joy Pittman

DAY 5

Rewards of Keeping the Faith

Scripture Focus:

"I have fought the good fight, I have finished the race, I have kept the faith. Now there is in store for me the crown of righteousness, which the Lord, the righteous Judge, will award to me on that day — not only to me but also to all who have longed for his appearing." (2 Timothy 4:7-8, NIV)

Let's Get Into It:

As we venture into the latter portion of Paul's letter to Timothy, we are greeted with imagery of finishing a race, a fight well-fought, and faith diligently kept. This portion of scripture encourages believers to remain steadfast, looking forward to the eternal rewards that come with perseverance and unswerving faith.

The journey of faith is often depicted as a race in the scriptures, a marathon that requires endurance, dedication, and focus on the prize that awaits us. The Bible is filled with testimonies of individuals who kept the faith against all odds, from Noah's unwavering faith in the face of mockery (Genesis 6-9) to Stephen, whose firm belief sustained him even in the face of death (Acts 7:54-60). These narratives bolster our resolve to run our race with grace and determination.

Let Us Pray:

"Dear Lord, I come to you today with hope, inspired by the joyful reward promised to those who remain faithful to Your call. I ask for the strength and endurance to stay true to this path, keeping my eyes fixed on the eternal joy that awaits.

Help me to carry out my daily tasks with a heart dedicated to serving You, eager to hear the words, "Well done, good and faithful servant." Let this promise spur me into action, fueling my determination to serve You with consistency and joy.

I lay this prayer before You, trusting in Your never-failing support and guidance.

In Jesus' mighty name, I pray. Amen."

As you continue through your day, find moments to re-empower yourself. Here are some prompts you can reflect and meditate on:

- Matthew 25:21, "Well done, good and faithful servant! You have been faithful with a few things;

I will put you in charge of many things. Come and share your master's happiness!" (NIV).

- Pray for the endurance to remain faithful, nurturing an eager anticipation for the divine rewards that God has in store for every believer who perseveres.

DAY 6

Faith and Patience

Scripture Focus:

"We do not want you to become lazy, but to imitate those who through faith and patience inherit what has been promised." (Hebrews 6:12, NIV)

Let's Get Into It:

In today's focal scripture, a critical component accompanying faith is underscored - patience. It's a reminder that our walk of faith is not a sprint but a long-distance run, where patience is not merely a virtue but a necessity. The intertwining of faith and patience paints a picture of a believer who, despite the trials and time frames, stands resolute, knowing that the promises of God are yes and amen.

Consider the story of Abraham, who waited patiently for the promise of a son, showcasing an exemplary level of patience coupled with faith (Genesis 17:15-19).

Similarly, the story of Job portrays incredible endurance and steadfastness even amidst unspeakable suffering (Job 1:21). These biblical examples beckon us to not grow weary but to foster a deep-seated patience that collaborates with our faith, moving towards the inheritance of God's promises.

Let Us Pray:

"Dear Heavenly Father, today, I come before You asking for the grace to cultivate patience in my life, patience that stands unwavering amidst trials and times of waiting. I understand that Your timing is perfect, and Your promises are sure.

Lord, instill in me a steadfast spirit that remains firm, grounded in the assurance that Your return is near. Help me to navigate the daily challenges with a heart anchored in Your word, constantly expecting the glorious manifestation of Your promises in my life.

I place this request before You, confident in Your power and willingness to mold me according to Your purpose.

In Jesus' strong name, I pray. Amen."

As you continue through your day, find moments to re-empower yourself. Here are some prompts you can reflect and meditate on:

- James 5:8: "You too, be patient and stand firm, because the Lord's coming is near." (NIV).

- Ask God for the grace to develop a robust and enduring patience that stands firm in faith, enabling you to witness the manifestation of His promises in your life.

Joy Pittman

DAY 7

God's Character as Our Foundation

Scripture Focus:

"As for God, his way is perfect: The Lord's word is flawless; he shields all who take refuge in him." (Psalms 18:30, NIV)

Let's Get Into It:

Today, we are focusing on recognizing and accepting God's unwavering and dependable character as the bedrock of our faith. Understanding that God's way is "perfect" and His word "flawless" guides us to place our complete trust in Him, not wavering even when circumstances prompt us to doubt.

Consider the numerous instances in the Bible where God proved Himself to be steadfast and reliable. In the face of Israelites' various trials during their journey to the promised land, God's character remained unchanging, providing them protection and guidance (Numbers 23:19). Our challenge then is to anchor our faith firmly on His unchangeable nature, allowing this knowledge to foster a deeper, more resilient faith.

Let Us Pray:

"Dear Lord, Thank you for being a consistent and steadfast force in my life, a beacon of hope and a wellspring of joy. I recognize that your name is a strong tower, a place of refuge where I can find peace and stability amidst the changing tides of life.

I come to you today, asking for the grace to continually find joy and stability in your unchanging character. Teach me to trust in you wholeheartedly, knowing that you never forsake those who earnestly seek you.

Lord, I rest in the assurance that as I grow to know you more, my trust in you will deepen, fostering a relationship that is grounded in your unfailing love and faithfulness.

I present this prayer before you, fully relying on your strength and grace to see me through.

In the mighty name of Jesus, I pray. Amen."

As you continue through your day, find moments to re-empower yourself. Here are some prompts you can reflect and meditate on:

- Psalms 9:10: "Those who know your name trust in you, for you, LORD, have never forsaken those who seek you." (NIV)

- Ask God to help you find joy and stability in God's steadfast character consistently.

Joy Pittman

Day 8

Facing Consequences of Faithlessness

Scripture Focus:

"Do not be deceived: God cannot be mocked. A man reaps what he sows. Whoever sows to please their flesh, from the flesh will reap destruction; whoever sows to please the Spirit, from the Spirit will reap eternal life." (Galatians 6:7-8, NIV)

Let's Get Into It:

On day 8, we are venturing into a critical yet often overlooked area of our spiritual journey: understanding the repercussions of faithlessness. In his letter to the Galatians, Paul is unambiguous about the inevitable consequences of sowing seeds of the flesh, which leads to destruction. Conversely, he highlights the immense rewards of sowing to please the Spirit.

This message should serve as both a warning and an encouragement to us. As we navigate life, we must be conscious of the seeds we sow daily. Sometimes, it is common to stray and give in to worldly pleasures and distractions. The Bible gives us many examples of individuals who faced the dire consequences of faithlessness, such as King Saul, whose disobedience led to his downfall (1 Samuel 15:23).

Let Us Pray:

"Dear Merciful Father, thank you for your unwavering faithfulness and your promise of purification that is ever present in your word. I stand in awe of your grace that readily embraces us, even when we falter and stray.

Today, I come before you with a repentant heart, earnestly seeking your forgiveness and cleansing from all unrighteousness. Lord, guide me in sowing seeds of righteousness in my daily walk, cultivating a landscape of goodness and mercy that mirrors your kingdom.

I pray for the strength to resist temptation and the wisdom to walk in paths that honor you. Lead me on a journey of continuous growth and sanctification, where my actions reflect a heart transformed by your love and grace.

I trust in your promise, Lord, that as I confess my shortcomings, you are faithful to forgive and purify me, setting me on a path of righteousness and peace. I place my reliance on your never-failing love to guide me each day.

In Jesus' powerful name, I pray. Amen."

As you continue through your day, find moments to re-empower yourself, keeping 1 John 1:9 in your heart.

- "If we confess our sins, he is faithful and just and will forgive us our sins and purify us from all unrighteousness." (NIV),

- Seek God's forgiveness and guidance, focusing on sowing seeds of righteousness.

Joy Pittman

DAY 9

The Joy of God's Presence

Scripture Focus:

"You make known to me the path of life; you will fill me with joy in your presence, with eternal pleasures at your right hand." (Psalms 16:11, NIV)

Let's Get Into It:

On this ninth day, we dive into the profound bliss and fulfillment found in God's presence. It is an understatement to say that life can sometimes be burdensome, and joy might seem elusive. Yet, today's scripture illuminates the unwavering source of true joy - the presence of God. It's a fleeting happiness and a fullness of perennial, deep, and fulfilling joy.

David, the psalmist, beautifully encapsulates the euphoria of being in God's presence, a place where, even amidst trials, an overwhelming sense of peace and happiness can be accessed. A similar sentiment is echoed in the story of Paul and Silas, who could sing praises joyfully in prison, witnessing the power of God's presence even in dire circumstances (Acts 16:25).

Let Us Pray:

"Dear Lord, thank you for your unending blessings and for the joy we find in Your presence.

Today, we come to you seeking a deeper connection with you, a connection that brings true peace and happiness into our lives. Lord, help us to fully comprehend and appreciate the security and joy that lies in being close to you.

We ask for the strength and wisdom to maintain this connection, so our lives can be a testament to the serene bliss and understanding found in Your presence.

We trust in Your promise, and in Your powerful name, we pray. Amen."

As you continue through your day, find moments to re-empower yourself. Here are some prompts you can reflect and meditate on:

- Psalms 21:6 - "Surely you have granted him unending blessings and made him glad with the joy of your presence." (NIV)

- Ask God for a greater revelation of His presence.

_____
_____
_____
_____
_____
_____
_____
_____
_____
_____
_____
_____
_____
_____
_____
_____
_____
_____
_____
_____
_____
_____
_____
_____
_____

DAY 10

Faith in Action

Scripture Focus:

"In the same way, faith by itself, if it is not accompanied by action, is dead." (James 2:17, NIV)

Let's Get Into It:

On this tenth day, we grapple with the fundamental concept that faith is not a passive belief but an active endeavor. It beckons us to move beyond mere words, putting our convictions into concrete actions that manifest God's love and righteousness. James, the author of this letter, doesn't mince words in emphasizing the futility of a faith not demonstrated through deeds.

Jesus showcased this through His earthly ministry; His actions always complemented His teachings. He healed, forgave, and loved actively (Matthew 9:35). Furthermore, He encouraged His followers to do likewise, to be the light of the world, letting their good deeds shine before others (Matthew 5:16). It's a call to practical, everyday Christianity, where our faith is continuously demonstrated through our actions.

Let Us Pray:

"Dear Heavenly Father, thank you for the guidance and wisdom that you continually pour into our lives.

Today, we earnestly ask for the courage and strength to live out our faith tangibly in all we say and do. Help us to embody Your teachings, so our actions become a living testimony of Your transformative power at work within us.

As we journey through each day, remind us to always give thanks and to honor You through our deeds, demonstrating Your grace and love to those around us.

In Your strong name, we pray. Amen."

As you continue through your day, find moments to re-empower yourself. Here are some prompts you can reflect and meditate on:

- Colossians 3:17 - "And whatever you do, whether in word or deed, do it all in the name of the Lord Jesus, giving thanks to God the Father through him." (NIV).

- As you meditate on this, pray for the courage and strength to consistently put your faith into actionable steps daily, serving as a vibrant testament to God's transformative power in your life.

_____
_____
_____
_____
_____
_____
_____
_____
_____
_____
_____
_____
_____
_____
_____
_____
_____
_____
_____
_____
_____
_____
_____
_____
_____
_____

DAY 11

Trusting God's Good Thoughts

Scripture Focus:

"For I know the plans I have for you," declares the LORD, "plans to prosper you and not to harm you, plans to give you hope and a future." (Jeremiah 29:11, NIV)

Let's Get Into It:

At times, the trials of life may blur our perception, causing us to question God's intentions toward us. Today, we delve deep into the profound assurance that God harbors benevolent thoughts for us, promising a horizon adorned with hope and prosperity. Jeremiah, speaking the words of the Lord, gives us a powerful promise that transcends time, a lifeline in moments of doubt and uncertainty.

We see numerous instances in the Bible where God unfolded His glorious plans in the lives of individuals who trusted Him. For instance, Joseph, who endured years of hardship, was ultimately elevated to a position of significant influence, showcasing God's good and redemptive plans (Genesis 50:20). In the New Testament, we witness the transformative journey of Saul to Paul, a testament to God's plan that can redirect and restore lives profoundly (Acts 9:1-19).

Let Us Pray:

"Dear God, we come before You with hearts filled with thanksgiving for Your steadfast love and guidance.

Today, we earnestly seek to deepen our trust in Your magnificent and good plans for us. Help us to resist the temptation to lean on our limited understanding, but instead immerse ourselves in Your boundless wisdom and enduring promises.

Guide us, O Lord, to surrender our plans and desires, choosing to wholly submit to Your divine will, knowing with confidence that You will lead us along the right paths.

In the powerful name of Jesus, we place our trust and hope. Amen."

As you continue through your day, find moments to re-empower yourself. Here are some prompts you can reflect and meditate on:

- Proverbs 3:5-6, "Trust in the LORD with all your heart and lean not on your own understanding; in all your ways submit to him, and he will make your paths straight." (NIV).

- Trust in God's plan for you, resolving not to lean on your fleeting understanding but on His enduring promises.

Count It All Joy

DAY 12

The Joy of Salvation

Scripture Focus:

"Restore to me the joy of your salvation and grant me a willing spirit, to sustain me." (Psalm 51:12, NIV)

Let's Get Into It:

The journey of faith is like navigating through diverse terrains, where, at times, the enthusiasm and joy we once had might wane. Today, we are invited to rediscover the boundless joy that salvation brings into our lives, a joy that rejuvenates and sustains us in our spiritual pilgrimage.

In the story of the Prodigal Son found in Luke 15:11-32, we witness the restoration and joy that embraces one who was lost but found his way back home. This narrative portrays the immense joy that is not just for the redeemed but also resonates in heaven. Rediscovering the joy of salvation is like reigniting a vital flame that brightens our spiritual pathway, granting us a renewed zest and eagerness in our relationship with God.

Let Us Pray:

"Dear Heavenly Father, we come before You with a spirit of gratitude, acknowledging Your redemptive power and grace in our lives.

Today, we seek a fresh infilling of Your joy, the deep, resounding joy that comes from salvation. We ask You to stir within us a spirit eager to embrace Your ways, adorned in the righteous robes You've lovingly bestowed upon us.

Lord, reignite our souls to rejoice in You continuously, finding our ultimate delight in Your presence and the beautiful journey of faith You have set before us.

We commit to walk in this joy and vibrancy daily, holding firm to our faith in You, trusting in Your capacity to uphold us in every season.

In the mighty name of Jesus, we pray. Amen."

As you continue through your day, find moments to re-empower yourself. Here are some prompts you can reflect and meditate on:

- Guided by the words of Isaiah 61:10, "I delight greatly in the LORD; my soul rejoices in my God. For he has clothed me with garments of salvation and arrayed me in a robe of his righteousness..." (NIV).

- Ask God fervently to restore the innate joy of salvation in us and to continually uphold us with a spirit willing to embrace His ways with vitality and happiness.

Day 13

Boldness in Faith

Scripture Focus:

"Let us then approach God's throne of grace with confidence, so that we may receive mercy and find grace to help us in our time of need." (Hebrews 4:16, NIV)

Let's Get Into It:

Embarking on a faith journey requires courage and a bold spirit. As we delve into today's scripture, we recognize the significant privilege we have to approach God's throne with confidence. This is not just a gentle encouragement to step closer, but a direct invitation to come as we are, with the assurance that we are valued and accepted by God.

Bold faith means fully relying on God's grace and mercy. Hebrews 4:16 suggests that when we approach God with confidence, we are met with mercy and grace, vital elements in our spiritual growth. This passage marks a significant shift from the Old Testament, where only high priests were allowed to approach God.

The Bible offers many examples of individuals demonstrating remarkable boldness in their faith. For instance, the woman with the issue of blood in Mark 5:25-34 showed immense faith in Jesus' healing power, braving the crowd just to touch His cloak.

Similarly, the Apostle Paul, as detailed in Acts 13 to 28, showcases a faith that was vocal and fearless, even in the face of adversity, constantly relying on God's grace and mercy.

Let Us Pray:

"Dear Heavenly Father, thank you for the freedom and confidence you have bestowed upon us, a precious gift that allows us to approach You with an open heart. We acknowledge Your unending goodness and grace that envelop us each day.

Today, we pray for a spirit that mirrors both boldness and humility, enabling us to seek You fervently and wholeheartedly. May we always come before You with eagerness, fully assured that You are ever ready to meet us at our point of need.

We trust in Your unfailing love and mercy, knowing that You are the source of all strength and peace. Help us to continually lean on You, with faith that does not waver, even in the face of trials.

In the strong name of Jesus, we pray. Amen."

As you continue through your day, find moments to re-empower yourself. Here are some prompts you can reflect and meditate on:

- Ephesians 3:12 - "In him and through faith in him we may approach God with freedom and confidence..." (NIV).

- Reflect and pray for a spirit that is both bold and humble, a spirit that seeks God's presence, armed with the assurance of His goodness and grace that always meets us at the point of our needs.

_____
_____
_____
_____
_____
_____
_____
_____
_____
_____
_____
_____
_____
_____
_____
_____
_____
_____
_____
_____
_____
_____
_____
_____
_____
_____
_____
_____

DAY 14

Faith that Overcomes

Scripture Focus:

"For everyone born of God overcomes the world. This is the victory that has overcome the world, even our faith." (1 John 5:4, NIV)

Let's Get Into It:

As we immerse ourselves in today's passage, we find ourselves at the intersection of struggle and victory. The scripture boldly declares a profound truth: our faith is not passive but rather a dynamic, vibrant force that has the power to overcome the world. This declaration does not come lightly, considering the numerous hurdles and trials that characterize life.

But what does it truly mean to have a faith that overcomes? It means acknowledging that our faith, rooted deeply in God's love and truth, equips us to face trials with resilience and courage. It means holding steadfastly to the belief that our victory is assured in Christ no matter the challenges. The Apostle John, who penned these words, had witnessed firsthand the life, death, and resurrection of Jesus Christ - the ultimate victory over the world.

To get a deeper understanding, we might look at examples in the Bible where faith demonstrated its overcoming power. In the Old Testament, we see individuals like Daniel, who, with unyielding faith, face the lions' den (Daniel 6) and emerge unharmed, showcasing the protective power of faith. In the New Testament, we observe the Apostles, who, despite persecution and trials, spread the gospel with unflinching courage, further extending the victory of faith across nations and generations.

Let us, therefore, gear up to live in this overcoming faith daily, seizing the victory that is already ours, courtesy of the firm foundation we have in Jesus Christ.

Let Us Pray:

"Dear Lord, thank you for your boundless love that has made us more than conquerors. We recognize that through you, victory is not just a possibility but a guarantee.

Today, we come before you, seeking the grace to embody this truth in every facet of our lives. Lord, grant us the strength and perseverance to face the trials and challenges that come our way, with the assurance that in You, we are already victorious.

May our hearts be steadfast, holding onto the promise that no matter the battles we face, Your love anchors us, making us more than conquerors. Help us to live out this truth daily, reflecting Your power and might in our lives.

In the mighty name of Jesus, we pray. Amen."

As you continue through your day, find moments to re-empower yourself. Here are some prompts you can reflect and meditate on:

- Romans 8:37 - "No, in all these things we are more than conquerors through him who loved us." (NIV), let us pray for the grace to truly live as conquerors.

- Ask God for the strength and perseverance to overcome life's challenges, leaning into the victorious power of steadfast faith.

_____

_____

_____

_____

_____

_____

_____

_____

_____

_____

_____

_____

_____

_____

_____

_____

_____

_____

_____

_____

_____

_____

_____

_____

_____

_____

_____

_____

_____

_____

DAY 15

The Gift of Peace

Scripture Focus:

"And the peace of God, which transcends all understanding, will guard your hearts and your minds in Christ Jesus." (Philippians 4:7, NIV)

Let's Get Into It:

Today, we venture into a territory often sought but scarcely found - peace. In a world rife with chaos, uncertainty, and strife, the scripture offers us an oasis, a peace that surpasses all human comprehension, anchored firmly in Christ Jesus.

But how do we tap into this profound peace? First, we must understand that this peace is not a product of external circumstances but springs from a deep relationship with Christ. It is a gift bestowed upon us, a beautiful consequence of entrusting our cares, worries, and fears unto God. The lesson here emphasizes the protective nature of God's peace – it guards our hearts and minds, two vital components that dictate our reactions to life's circumstances.

We find the perfect embodiment of this peace in Jesus Christ, who, amidst storms, could sleep peacefully in the boat (Mark 4:35-41), showcasing a deep-seated tranquility rooted in His unity with the Father. Similarly, as we nurture our relationship with God, we can experience this same peace, an inner calm that remains unshaken, irrespective of the storms that rage around us.

Drawing deeper from the well of scripture, we can juxtapose this with the calming reassurance Jesus imparted to His disciples in John 14:27, "Peace I leave with you; my peace I give you. I do not give to you as the world gives. Do not let your hearts be troubled, and do not be afraid."

Let Us Pray:

"Dear Heavenly Father, we are profoundly grateful for the peace that You offer, a peace that transcends all understanding, a peace that the world cannot give.

Today, we come before You earnestly seeking this peace to be a steadfast presence in our lives. In moments where chaos seems to prevail, remind us, Lord, to lean into Your unfailing grace, where our hearts and minds can find rest and tranquility.

We ask for the grace to be open vessels, ready to receive and bask in Your divine peace. In the midst of life's turbulent waves, may Your peace be our anchor, steadying us and offering solace and stability.

We place our trust in You, confident that as we seek You, we will find the peace that You promised, a peace that is everlasting and unshakeable.

In the strong name of Jesus, we pray. Amen."

As you continue through your day, find moments to re-empower yourself. Here are some prompts you can reflect and meditate on:

- John 14:27. Let's approach God with a fervent desire for His peace, the peace that calms storms and guards hearts and minds.

- Pray for grace to be receptive to this divine peace.

_____

_____

_____

_____

_____

_____

_____

_____

_____

_____

_____

_____

_____

_____

_____

_____

_____

_____

_____

_____

_____

_____

_____

_____

_____

DAY 16

Obedience and Its Rewards

Scripture Focus:

"If you are willing and obedient, you will eat the good things of the land;" (Isaiah 1:19, NIV).

Let's Get Into It:

Today, we delve into a theme as ancient as humankind – obedience. From the early narratives of the Bible, obedience to God's commandments has stood as a pillar of a blessed and prosperous life. In a world that often promotes self-sufficiency and rebellion, God calls us to a higher standard – a life of willing obedience to His commands.

The nuances of 'willing obedience' are worth pondering. It isn't just about compliance but a readiness of the heart, a keen eagerness to align with God's precepts. This distinction is vital, transforming acts of obedience from mere duty to a joyous endeavor. It signals a mature and loving relationship with God, where we obey not out of fear but in love and reverence for Him.

A deeper dive into scripture reveals a harmonious correlation between obedience and blessings. In Deuteronomy 28:1-2, we observe a vivid depiction of the abundant rewards that trail the path of obedience: "If you fully obey the Lord your God and carefully follow all his commands I give you today, the Lord your God will set you high above all the nations on earth. All these blessings will come on you and accompany you if you obey the Lord your God."

Let Us Pray:

"Dear Heavenly Father, as I pause today, I meditate on the profound promises in Deuteronomy 28:1-2. I come before You with a sincere heart, seeking Your enabling grace to guide me in daily obedience to Your will.

Lord, I desire to cultivate a heart that is eager to heed Your commands, fostering a relationship with You that is based on deep reverence and love. Lead me, Father, so that each step I take aligns with Your divine plans, permitting me to embrace the abundance of blessings You have prepared for me.

May my life be a vibrant testament to Your goodness, reflecting the prosperity and favor that stem from obedience to Your word. I pray that day by day, I grow more attuned to Your voice, walking faithfully in the path You have set before me.

In the strong name of Jesus, I pray. Amen."

As you continue through your day, find moments to re-empower yourself. Here are some prompts you can reflect and meditate on:

- Deuteronomy 28:1-2. Let's approach God with a sincere heart.

- Seek His grace to empower you to walk daily in willing obedience, thereby stepping into the fullness of blessings He has in store for those who heed His commands.

DAY 17

The Dangers of Disobedience

Scripture Focus:

"Whoever keeps commandments keeps their life, but whoever shows contempt for their ways will die." (Proverbs 19:16, NIV)

Let's Get Into It:

In the realms of spiritual journeying, the path of disobedience is treacherous, often leading to repercussions that extend beyond the transient moments of rebellion. Today's lesson draws us back to the wisdom-laden book of Proverbs, urging us to consider the gravity of straying from God's decrees.

Disobedience, often birthed from a place of pride, self-reliance, or mistrust, tends to isolate us from the protective canopy of God's guidance and blessings. It breeds turmoil, a disconnect from the divine harmony that God intends for us. Moreover, it fosters a landscape where the enemy finds room to operate, creating footholds that can lead to greater spiritual downfall.

To illuminate the dangers further, we can take a cue from numerous biblical narratives that recount the dire consequences of disobedience. For instance, the story of King Saul in 1 Samuel 15 paints a vivid picture of how disobedience can lead to personal loss and the forfeiture of God's blessings and favor. It serves as a cautionary tale, beckoning us to adhere to God's instructions meticulously.

Let Us Pray:

"Dear God, today, I come to You with a humble heart, asking for the wisdom and courage to avoid the path of disobedience. Help me to hold Your teachings close to my heart, serving as a shield against any wrongdoings.

I ask for Your guidance in fostering a strong determination to follow Your path, steering clear of mistakes and missteps that come from not listening to Your word. Help me to live a life that is pleasing to You, protecting me from falling into the traps that disobedience brings.

I pray for this grace and guidance, trusting wholly in Your unfailing support.

In Jesus' powerful name, I pray. Amen."

As you continue through your day, find moments to re-empower yourself. Here are some prompts you can reflect and meditate on:

- Psalms 119:11, "I have hidden your word in my heart that I might not sin against you".

- Seek to embed God's word in your heart to avoid the pitfalls that disobedience brings.

DAY 18

Rejoicing in Hope

Scripture Focus:

"Be joyful in hope, patient in affliction, faithful in prayer." (Romans 12:12, NIV)

Let's Get Into It:

As we step into today's lesson, we find ourselves standing on the fertile grounds of hope—where joy, patience, and faithfulness converge to create a sanctuary of spiritual nourishment. Romans 12:12 encapsulates a brief but potent blueprint for living a Christian life that vibrates with positivity and resilience.

The joy from harboring hope in Christ is unlike any earthly happiness. It's a kind of joy that is unfazed by external circumstances, rooted deeply in the knowledge of the eternal promises that God has made to us. This joy propels us to remain patient, even when facing tribulations, for our hope in Christ is steadfast and unmovable.

But how do we nurture this hope and let it bloom in fullness within us? The latter part of the scripture gives us a hint - by being faithful in prayer. Prayer is the channel through which we continually align ourselves with God's promises, fostering a relationship that breeds trust and hope.

To further grasp this, we can reflect on the story of Abraham in Romans 4:18-20. Despite the hopelessness of his circumstances, he chose to hope in God's promises, his faith not wavering. Abraham's life serves as a vibrant testament to the kind of hope birthed from a deep, unyielding faith in God, a hope that transcends human understanding and limitations.

Let Us Pray:

"Dear God, today, I come before You with a heart eager to remain steadfast in hope. Guide me to continually find joy and assurance in Your promises. Let my spirit be ever vibrant, filled with hope and an unyielding joy that magnifies Your presence in my life.

Help me to embrace a spirit that constantly seeks to praise You, finding new reasons to celebrate Your goodness each day. As I navigate through life, let my hope in You be the anchor that holds me steady, encouraging me to praise You more and more with each passing day.

I trust in Your unfailing love to nurture this hope within me, leaning on Your enduring promises for strength and joy.

In Jesus' mighty name, I pray. Amen."

As you continue through your day, find moments to re-empower yourself. Here are some prompts you can reflect and meditate on:

- Focus towards the commitment of remaining steadfast in hope Psalms 71:14 - "As for me, I will always have hope; I will praise you more and more"

- Meditate on and rejoice in the promises of God.

Count It All Joy

Day 19

The Joy of Giving

Scripture Focus:

"In everything I did, I showed you that by this kind of hard work, we must help the weak, remembering the words the Lord Jesus himself said: 'It is more blessed to give than to receive.'" (Acts 20:35, NIV)

Let's Get Into It:

Today, we venture into the enriching world of giving, a world painted with hues of generosity and genuine joy. In the book of Acts, Paul reminded the elders at Ephesus of the profound words of Jesus, drawing attention to the deep-seated joy derived from giving, a principle that forms the bedrock of a fulfilling Christian life.

At the core of giving is a heart that desires the welfare and happiness of others, even at the cost of personal sacrifice. But we often overlook the transformative power this act holds, not only for those we give to but also within us. As we give, we align ourselves with God's nature, for He is the ultimate giver who gave His only Son to redeem humanity.

It's critical to underline that giving extends beyond material possessions. It encapsulates the giving of our love, knowledge, and our forgiveness to others. By embracing a lifestyle of giving, we become vessels through which God's love and blessings flow unceasingly.

Consider the story of the widow's offering in Mark 12:41-44. Despite her limited resources, her act of giving was significant in the eyes of Jesus, showcasing that the true essence of giving lies in the heart, not in the magnitude of what is given.

Let Us Pray:

"Dear Father, today, I stand before You, seeking to cultivate a heart that reflects Your generous and loving nature. I ask You to infuse within me a spirit that delights in giving, that finds pure joy in sharing blessings with others.

Guide me, Lord, to give not out of obligation or reluctance but from a place of genuine happiness and willingness. Shape my heart to be more like Yours, a heart that gives cheerfully, echoing Your boundless love and generosity.

Lord, help me to make decisions rooted in love and kindness, always eager to contribute to the well-being of others with a cheerful spirit.

I trust You to lead me in this journey, fostering a generous heart that brings joy to both the giver and the receiver.

In the powerful name of Jesus, I pray. Amen."

As you continue through your day, find moments to re-empower yourself. Here are some prompts you can reflect and meditate on:

- Reflect on the essence of being a cheerful giver as described in 2 Corinthians 9:7

- Take a few moments to meditate on the joy that comes with giving cheerfully. As you meditate, ask God to reveal to you the areas where you can embrace this spirit of joyful giving more fully, transforming your heart to mirror His generosity and love.

Count It All Joy

_____

_____

_____

_____

_____

_____

_____

_____

_____

_____

_____

_____

_____

_____

_____

_____

_____

_____

_____

_____

_____

_____

_____

_____

_____

DAY 20

Growing in Faith

Scripture Focus:

"We ought always to thank God for you, brothers and sisters, and rightly so, because your faith is growing more and more, and the love all of you have for one another is increasing." (2 Thessalonians 1:3, NIV)

Let's Get Into It:

Today's topic highlights the ongoing journey of faith—a journey that is active and continuously evolving. Faith isn't something that stays static; it's something we develop daily as we deepen our relationship with God and with the people around us.

A robust faith is noticeable in our actions, the way we speak, and how we treat others. As we move forward, it's our duty to nurture our faith and to recognize and support the growing faith we see in other believers. Doing this not only builds a community but showcases the genuine appreciation that we should naturally carry within us.

Looking at the example of the Thessalonians, we see a group deeply rooted in mutual respect and thankfulness for the evident growth in faith and love in their community. This growth isn't isolated but linked to an increase in love for one another, clearly showing the undeniable relationship between growing in faith and increasing in love.

Let Us Pray:

"Dear God, I come before you today, eager to grow more into the likeness of Jesus Christ, your beloved Son. I acknowledge the journey of spiritual growth can sometimes be difficult, and I admit that I sometimes stumble.

Please guide me in my daily walk, helping me to embody love and kindness in all I do. Let your words deeply influence my actions and my speech, allowing me to reflect your light and love in this world.

Grant me the patience and resilience to navigate life's challenges and to foster relationships that glorify your name. I seek your wisdom, Lord, to grow and flourish in your grace.

I entrust this journey to you, fully relying on your guidance and looking forward to the beautiful transformation unfolding in my life. In the strong name of Jesus, I pray. Amen."

As you continue through your day, find moments to re-empower yourself. Here are some prompts you can reflect and meditate on:

- Reflect on Ephesians 4:15. Ponder on the areas in your life where you aspire to embody more of Christ's attributes.

- In your quiet moments today, ask God for wisdom and guidance in nurturing growth in those areas.

DAY 21

The Essence of Community

Scripture Focus:

"And let us consider how we may spur one another on toward love and good deeds, not giving up meeting together, as some are in the habit of doing, but encouraging one another — and all the more as you see the Day approaching." (Hebrews 10:24-25, NIV)

Let's Get Into It:

In today's world, it's common to focus on oneself, but the scripture we're looking at today reminds us of the importance of community. Being part of a community isn't just about coming together; it's about actively encouraging each other to love and do good things for others.

The foundation of a strong community is the shared goal of pushing each other towards greater levels of love and helping others. The scripture from Hebrews describes a united group of people coming together not just to meet, but to inspire love and encourage positive actions.

Being part of a community provides a safe space where people can find support and the inspiration to keep going, especially as we look forward to the Day of the Lord. It's a place where faith grows, relationships are strengthened, and the process of becoming more holy is a shared experience.

Let's reflect on these verses and aim to take an active role in our communities, using our special talents to enhance the well-being and development of the group as a whole.

Let Us Pray:

"Dear Heavenly Father, thank you for the gift of community and the joy that comes from uplifting one another. I come to you today asking for the wisdom and heart to be someone who encourages and builds others up. Grant me the sensitivity to see the needs of those around me, and the zeal to foster unity and love in my community. Help me to actively participate in nurturing bonds that are strong, uplifting, and reflective of Your love.

I also come before You with a repentant heart, acknowledging the times I have failed to be a source of encouragement. Forgive me for the moments when I have focused more on myself, missing the opportunities to uplift others. Guide me so that I can be a better vessel of Your grace and love.

I firmly believe that with Your guidance, I can be transformed to be more like You each day. As I step forward, may I do so in the strong name of Jesus, Amen."

As you continue through your day, find moments to re-empower yourself. Here are some prompts you can reflect and meditate on:

- 1 Thessalonians 5:11, "Therefore encourage one another and build each other up, just as in fact you are doing."

- Seek God's guidance to become an agent of encouragement, fostering a community that is united in love, ever eager to uplift and build each other up in faith and good works.

DAY 22

The Blessings of Obedience

Scripture Focus:

"If you fully obey the Lord your God and carefully follow all his commands I give you today, the Lord your God will set you high above all the nations on earth. All these blessings will come on you and accompany you if you obey the Lord your God..." (Deuteronomy 28:1-14, NIV)

Let's Get Into It:

In today's passage, the message is clear: following God's rules brings blessings into our lives. This scripture paints a hopeful picture of the good things that come our way when we listen to God and follow His guidance.

These blessings can touch every part of our lives, including our finances, family relationships, and personal health. When we choose to follow God's rules, we put ourselves in a place where we can fully receive

His favor and good things without end. This place of favor elevates us, showcasing the good that comes from living an obedient life.

However, it's important to remember that the goal of obedience isn't just to receive blessings; it's a way to show our love and respect for God. It's a visible sign of the inner changes happening within us, indicating a soul that's in sync with what God wants. As we think about this passage, let's try to understand the depth of the blessings promised and aim to follow God's commands, not just for the rewards, but more importantly, to deepen our connection with Him and to find joy in doing what pleases Him.

Let Us Pray:

"Dear Lord, thank you for your constant presence and love in my life. I am grateful for the numerous blessings you shower upon me each day.

I come to you now, asking for the courage and strength to always respect and follow your will. Sometimes I stray and fail to do what you ask of me. Forgive me for those times and help guide me back to the path of obedience. I desire to have a heart that is open to your commands, welcoming the rich blessings that come with being faithful to you.

Lord, mold me into someone who not only listens to your word but lives it out daily. Help me to walk in step with your plans for me, knowing that your way is the best way.

I declare this prayer, believing in your mighty power to transform my life, in the strong name of Jesus, Amen."

As you continue through your day, find moments to re-empower yourself. Here are some prompts you can reflect and meditate on:

- Psalms 128:1, which says, "Blessed are all who fear the Lord, who walk in obedience to him,"

- Pray for the grace and strength to walk in reverence and obedience to God.

Count It All Joy

DAY 23

The Call to Servanthood

Scripture Focus:

"For even the Son of Man did not come to be served, but to serve, and to give his life as a ransom for many." (Mark 10:45, NIV)

Let's Get Into It:

Today, we're exploring the concept of servanthood, inspired by Jesus, the ultimate servant leader. Today's scripture highlights the core of servanthood: humility, selflessness, and a genuine desire to uplift others.

This call urges us to move away from self-focused approaches and to find joy in serving others in small, everyday ways. Jesus' time on earth was defined by acts that healed and uplifted many, setting a standard for us to be more tuned into the needs around us, becoming vessels of God's love and grace.

As we strive to grasp the essence of servanthood, let's aspire to mirror Jesus, seizing daily opportunities to serve others with a heart full of humility and love. Remember, in God's eyes, the true leader is the one who serves all.

Let Us Pray:

"Dear Lord, thank you for the inspiring example of Jesus, who led with love and humility, always putting others first.

I ask now for a heart like His, one that finds joy in serving others without expecting anything in return. Forgive me for the times I've let selfish ambition guide my actions. Transform me, Lord, into a true servant, valuing others above myself and looking out for the interests of others.

Help me to embody this spirit of servanthood daily, reflecting the selflessness and love that Jesus demonstrated so perfectly during His time on earth.

I pray all this, trusting in the strong name of Jesus, Amen."

As you continue through your day, find moments to re-empower yourself. Here are some prompts you can reflect and meditate on:

- Philippians 2:3-4 urges us to "do nothing out of selfish ambition or vain conceit. Rather, in humility value others above yourselves, not looking to your interests but each of you to the interests of the others,"

- Pray for a servant's heart that echoes Jesus' humility and love.

Count It All Joy

_____
_____
_____
_____
_____
_____
_____
_____
_____
_____
_____
_____
_____
_____
_____
_____
_____
_____
_____
_____
_____
_____
_____
_____
_____
_____

DAY 24

Rekindling the Joy

Scripture Focus:

"When anxiety was great within me, your consolation brought me joy." (Psalm 94:19, NIV)

Let's Get Into It:

In our faith journey, there are times when joy seems distant, overshadowed by stress, worry, and daily pressures. However, our happiness isn't tied to these external factors but is rooted in God's unchanging nature and promises.

Today, we focus on reigniting joy even in difficult times. This is not a passive experience; it involves actively seeking happiness and making sure it remains alive even in the face of challenges. It's about continually returning to God, the source of our joy, and finding peace in His presence that goes beyond all understanding.

This process of finding joy in God's promises changes us. It means digging into God's word and holding on to His promises of endless love, care, and peace. It's a deliberate choice to see the good in situations, to be thankful, and to find comfort in the small joyful moments God gives us each day.

In hard times, we need to focus less on the problems and more on God, who can bring peace amidst chaos. Because being with Him brings a kind of joy that isn't affected by worldly troubles, a joy that refreshes and heals our spirit.

Let Us Pray:

"Thank you, Lord, for always being a source of joy and strength in our lives. We are immensely grateful for Your steadfast love and the promises that anchor our spirits.

Father, we find ourselves in moments where joy seems distant, and we earnestly ask for Your help to renew our sense of joy. In times of distress, may we find our solace in You, leaning on Your promises that never fail. Forgive us for the times we have allowed our circumstances to dim the joy that resides in us through Your spirit.

We ask that You transform our mourning into moments of joy, granting us the ability to see beauty even in the midst of ashes. Fill our hearts with the oil of joy, enabling us to stand firm and resilient, grounded in Your love and grace.

We trust that You hear our prayer and will grant us this grace, for we ask in the strong name of Jesus, Amen."

As you continue through your day, find moments to re-empower yourself. Here are some prompts you can reflect and meditate on:

- Isaiah 61:3, Asks God to bestow upon us "a crown of beauty instead of ashes, the oil of joy instead of mourning."

- Seek God's face fervently, asking Him to renew our joy, to be our stronghold in times of distress, and to enable us to find happiness and solace in His promises.

Count It All Joy

_____
_____
_____
_____
_____
_____
_____
_____
_____
_____
_____
_____
_____
_____
_____
_____
_____
_____
_____
_____
_____
_____
_____
_____
_____
_____
_____
_____

Day 25

Faith that Moves Mountains

Scripture Focus:

He replied, "Because you have so little faith. Truly I tell you, if you have faith as small as a mustard seed, you can say to this mountain, 'Move from here to there,' and it will move. Nothing will be impossible for you." (Matthew 17:20, NIV)

Let's Get Into It:

The realm of faith is where the finite meets the infinite, where our human capabilities encounter divine possibilities. Today, we are reminded that our faith, even if as minuscule as a mustard seed, holds the potential to move mountains, to make a way where there seems to be no way. This kind of faith does not rely on what is visible to the human eye but clings steadfastly to the assurances of God's word.

In a world that often demands physical evidence, sustaining such strong faith can sometimes be challenging. It calls for a deep-rooted belief in the power of God, a trust that He is able to accomplish exceedingly, abundantly above all we ask or think. It is a dynamic faith that steps out, even when the path ahead is unclear, believing that God will pave the way.

As we venture into deeper realms of faith, we learn to lean not on our own understanding but to acknowledge God in all our ways. It's about recognizing that our God is not confined by the limitations of our human comprehension; He is a God of impossibilities, who commands mountains to move and pathways to appear in the wilderness. It is the kind of faith that looks at a closed door and still believes in opening grander gates.

Let Us Pray:

"Lord, thank you for being with me always, providing a foundation of faith in my life.

Today, I come to you with a simple request: to help me build a stronger, unyielding faith, a faith that trusts in Your power completely, even when I face huge obstacles. Forgive me for the times when my faith has wavered.

Please give me the courage and strength to believe in Your ability to work miracles in my life, and to move the mountains that stand in my way. Help me to remain steadfast, to keep my faith from faltering.

I place this request before You, trusting in the strong name of Jesus, Amen."

As you continue through your day, find moments to re-empower yourself. Here are some prompts you can reflect and meditate on:

- 1 Corinthians 13:2, seek to have a faith that can move mountains.

- Pray for faith that does not waver, and that firmly trusts in God's ability to move mountains in your life.

DAY 26

The Path of Righteousness

Scripture Focus:

"But the path of the righteous is like the light of dawn, which shines brighter and brighter until full day." (Proverbs 4:18, ESV)

Let's Get Into It:

Starting on the road to doing what's right is like setting out on a journey that leads us from the early morning light to the bright sunlight of noon. This picture from the book of Proverbs shows us that being a Christian means we're always moving forward, always growing and getting better, guided by the increasing light of God's truth and kindness.

Being on this journey means we need to be committed and keep going, even when it gets tough. But the great thing is, as we keep going, our relationship with God gets deeper and better. We find ourselves surrounded by His kindness and making wise choices. It's about building a relationship with God that keeps getting stronger and brighter, just like the morning sun grows into full daylight.

As we go further on this road, we start understanding what God wants from us more clearly. That doesn't mean it'll always be easy, but God's light will always be there to guide us through the hard times, giving us a kind of grace and understanding that goes beyond what we can explain.

Let Us Pray:

"Dear Heavenly Father, thank you for your never-ending love and grace. Today, we focus our hearts on Psalm 23:3, turning to you to guide us to always do what is right, making our lives a shining example of Your grace and magnificence.

We pray for the wisdom to recognize the right paths in front of us and the courage to walk them. We put our trust in You to lead us, relying on Your grace to help us grow and thrive under Your nurturing light.

Help us to stray not from the righteous path, allowing our journeys to always reflect Your glory. In moments of uncertainty, be our guiding force, pushing us towards actions that glorify Your name.

In the strong name of Jesus, we pray. Amen."

As you continue through your day, find moments to re-empower yourself. Here are some prompts you can reflect and meditate on:

- Psalm 23:3. Consider the implications of walking "unerringly on the path of righteousness".

- Take a moment to meditate on the concept of relying on God's grace to guide your journey. Visualize yourself walking a path illuminated by His grace, empowering you to grow and flourish.

DAY 27

Celebrating God's Faithfulness

Scripture Focus:

"The steadfast love of the Lord never ceases; his mercies never come to an end; they are new every morning; great is your faithfulness." (Lamentations 3:22-23, ESV)

Let's Get Into It:

It's easy to get caught up in the whirlwind of life's challenges, where the immediacies of our circumstances can sometimes cloud our vision. However, this day invites us to anchor ourselves firmly in the unfailing faithfulness of God. Every morning, as the sun rises, we are graced with a fresh batch of mercies from our Heavenly Father, a testament to His inexhaustible and unchanging faithfulness.

To celebrate God's faithfulness is to dwell in the shelter of His love, acknowledging that even when we are not steadfast, He remains constant, His mercies resplendent and renewing. It's a celebration that infuses our spirits with hope, instilling a joy that transcends our external circumstances.

In today's lesson, we take a moment to lift our eyes from our situations to behold the grandeur of God's faithfulness that stretches across time and space. It is to immerse ourselves in the euphoria of His love that never gives up, never runs dry, and that we are always ready to embrace ourselves with fresh opportunities to experience His grace anew.

Let Us Pray:

"Heavenly Father, I start this day with a heart brimming with gratitude for Your never-ending faithfulness that surrounds me at every moment. I am in awe of Your boundless love and mercy that renews with each day, a beacon of hope and a promise of Your steadfast presence in my life.

Lord, I pray that You nurture in me a heart that remains unswerving in this beautiful truth. Help me to blossom and grow under Your nurturing grace, to not only receive Your daily mercies but to extend them to those around me. Forgive me, Lord, for the times I have faltered, and guide me back onto the path of righteousness and compassion.

I stand on the promises of Your unfailing love, holding firm to my faith in the journey ahead, believing in the transformative power of Your grace in my life. I proclaim this in the strong name of Jesus, Amen."

As you continue through your day, find moments to re-empower yourself. Here are some prompts you can reflect and meditate on:

- Psalm 36:5. Consider how His love and mercy have been evident in your life.

- Spend a few moments meditating on the imagery of blossoming under the "gentle showers of His daily mercies". Visualize yourself growing and flourishing under God's nurturing care.

DAY 28

Standing Firm in Faith

Scripture Focus:

"Be on your guard; stand firm in the faith; be courageous; be strong." (1 Corinthians 16:13, NIV)

Let's Get Into It:

The faith journey is indeed beautiful yet challenging. It's a path that demands resilience, courage, and unwavering commitment to the foundations of our belief in God. In a world that sometimes appears to shake the very core of our convictions, standing firm in faith is not only a command but a necessity.

Today's lesson urges us to be vigilant and to guard our hearts and minds against influences that seek to destabilize our faith. It is a clarion call to exhibit courage, to be stalwarts who are not swayed by the ebbs and flows of societal tides. Standing firm in faith fosters a spiritual robustness that can withstand trials and tribulations, allowing us to remain rooted in the teachings and promises of God's word.

As believers, we are encouraged to adopt an attitude of spiritual fortitude, continually drawing strength from our relationship with God. Being strong in the Lord means relying on His might and allowing His Spirit to empower and encourage us daily.

Let Us Pray:

"Lord, I come before you today with a thankful heart, appreciating Your eternal presence and guidance in my life. Your love and wisdom have been my fortress, granting me peace amidst the storms.

Now, I seek Your divine strength, oh Lord, to be resilient in my faith, especially in challenging times. Inspired by the teachings in Ephesians, I pray for the courage to stand firm, fully clad in the armor You provide, showcasing Your glory through my life. I repent for the moments of weakness, where I may have faltered and not fully relied on Your strength. Grant me the grace to remain unshaken, grounded firmly in the truth of Your word.

I declare my trust in Your unwavering support and promise to guide me through every circumstance, reflecting Your glory in all that I do. I pray this with a heart full of faith, in the strong name of Jesus, Amen."

As you continue through your day, find moments to re-empower yourself. Here are some prompts you can reflect and meditate on:

- Ephesians 6:13, Reflect on the different components of the armor of God.

- Consider how each piece can practically help you to stand firm in your faith amidst challenges.

Day 29

The Rewards of Perseverance

Scripture Focus:

"Blessed is the one who perseveres under trial because, having stood the test, that person will receive the crown of life that the Lord has promised to those who love Him." (James 1:12, NIV)

Let's Get Into It:

Perseverance, an essential virtue in the life of a believer, is likened to a flame that continues to flicker even in the face of fierce winds. The resilient spirit refuses to be quieted, irrespective of the trials and tribulations that assail us. Today, we delve into the heart of perseverance, understanding that it is more than just a passive waiting but an active endurance, a continuous striving towards God's promises.

The journey of faith is indeed a marathon and not a sprint. It can embody a spirit of resilience, to hold on to our faith with a grip that does not waver, even when the storms of life rage against us. It beckons us to forge ahead, eyes fixed on the ultimate reward: the crown of life, a representation of eternal life, and the unbroken fellowship with our Creator.

Let Us Pray:

"Heavenly Father, we begin this day with a heart filled with gratitude for Your constant presence and guidance in our lives. Thank You for Your endless love and the blessings You bestow upon us each day.

As we navigate through the trials of life, we seek Your grace to persevere, drawing strength from the teachings in Galatians. Lord, empower us with a spirit that does not tire in pursuing goodness, and a heart that remains focused on the blessings that You promise to those who endure. We repent for the times we have faltered, giving in to weariness and doubt. Rekindle in us a resilient and hopeful spirit, keenly anticipating the glorious rewards that await us.

We stand firm in this prayer, trusting in Your promise to sustain us, and lead us to a life that is abundant and fulfilling, in the strong name of Jesus, Amen."

As you continue through your day, find moments to re-empower yourself. Here are some prompts you can reflect and meditate on:

- Galatians 6:9. How you can embody the spirit of perseverance and goodness in your daily life.

- Engage in a moment of meditation, focusing on nurturing a resilient spirit that remains hopeful and steadfast amidst trials. Picture yourself embracing the blessings that God promises to those who endure and ponder on the profound joy and peace that await in fulfilling God's call to perseverance and righteousness.

Count It All Joy

DAY 30

Embracing God's Joy

Scripture Focus:

"These things I have spoken to you, that my joy may be in you, and that your joy may be full." (John 15:11, ESV)

Let's Get Into It:

In the bustling busyness of life, where various challenges and distractions constantly tug at us, embracing God's joy may sometimes seem like an elusive quest. Yet, as we stand at the threshold of this spiritual journey, it is imperative to understand that the joy God offers transcends circumstantial happiness. It is a deep-seated joy rooted in the love and promises that emanate from a relationship with Him.

God's joy is not fleeting or dependent on external factors. It is a steady, unshakeable force that sustains us, even amid turmoil. This joy is intricately connected to our abiding in God's love and His Word, a holy intertwining that brings forth a fullness of joy that the world cannot give nor take away.

Let Us Pray:

"Dear Heavenly Father, we come to You with hearts full of thanksgiving, appreciating the infinite joy and peace that resides in Your presence. Thank you for being our ever-present source of hope and for the love that you shower upon us each day.

As we seek to grow closer to You, we ask You to fill us abundantly with joy and peace that transcends all understanding, nurturing our trust in You. We repent for the times we may have wavered in our faith and allowed worldly concerns to dim the joy that comes from being in Your presence. Guide us, Lord, to be vessels that overflow with the hope, joy, and peace that stems from a deep trust in You.

We declare this prayer with a fervent heart, believing in Your power to transform us into beacons of joy and peace in this world, in the strong name of Jesus, Amen."

As you continue through your day, find moments to re-empower yourself. Here are some prompts you can reflect and meditate on:

- Romans 15:13. Consider what it means to fully trust in God.

- Imagine yourself being a vessel that is continuously filled with God's love and peace. Allow this to shift your mindset about some of the challenges and life situations you face.

_____

_____

_____

_____

_____

_____

_____

_____

_____

_____

_____

_____

_____

_____

_____

_____

_____

_____

_____

_____

_____

_____

_____

_____

_____

_____

_____

Day 31

Reflecting and Moving Forward

Scripture Focus:

"Brothers, I do not consider that I have made it my own. But one thing I do: forgetting what lies behind and straining forward to what lies ahead, I press on toward the goal for the prize of the upward call of God in Christ Jesus." (Philippians 3:13-14, ESV)

Let's Get Into It:

As we wrap up this journey, it's important to take a moment to assess the progress we've made on our faith journey. This isn't just a time for reflection, but also a time for preparation as we gear up to face new challenges and opportunities to grow in our walk with God. It's vital to understand that this journey is ongoing, urging us to continuously cultivate our knowledge and understanding, always reaching for the higher calling in Christ Jesus.

It's not a sprint - it's a marathon, characterized by persistence and a steadfast focus on the ultimate goal: a deeper relationship with God. During this time, it's necessary to embrace patience and endurance, qualities that will help us navigate through the complexities of life. It means not getting bogged down by past failures or disappointments, but also not resting too long on past successes. Every day is a new opportunity to stretch ourselves further, to strive with renewed energy toward the wealth and depth that our relationship with God can offer.

As we move forward, let's actively decide to let go of the burdens from the past that may be holding us back and free ourselves to more fully embrace the present and the blessings it brings. Be encouraged to remain excited and passionate about our spiritual journey, eager to discover the profound depths of love, grace, and wisdom that are found in a committed walk with God. Let's step into the new place with fervent zeal, eyes fixed on the prize that awaits us in Christ Jesus.

Let Us Pray:

"Gracious God, thank you for guiding us every step of the way, and for the growth and lessons that have marked our journey so far. Your grace has been our steady companion, and for this, we are truly grateful.

As we stand at the brink of a fresh start, we humbly come before You, asking for the strength and wisdom to let go of all the hindrances and missteps that easily entangle us. Teach us, Lord, to run this race with perseverance, always keeping our gaze fixed on Jesus, who is the source and the goal of our faith.

Help us to be keen in recognizing the areas where we falter and quick in turning back to the path you've laid before us. Renew in us a steadfast spirit that is eager to honor you in all that we do.

We trust that with your guidance, we will walk this path with grace, demonstrating your love and light in our lives, and reflecting Jesus in our actions and choices.

In the strong name of Jesus, we pray, Amen."

As you continue through your day, find moments to re-empower yourself. Here are some prompts you can reflect and meditate on:

- Philippians 3:13-14. Consider how you can embody the teachings of pressing forward, leaving behind the past, and striving towards the prize promised in a life united with Christ.

- Take a moment to meditate on the notion of the spiritual journey being a marathon and not a sprint, as mentioned in the message. Visualize yourself releasing the weight of past disappointments and embracing the opportunities that each new day brings. Picture how you can cultivate patience, endurance, and an eagerness to grow in your relationship with

God. During this meditation, ponder on how you can maintain a fervent zeal in your spiritual journey, constantly reaching for the richness and depth that walking with God offers.

Closing Thoughts:

Hey Friend,

We've made it to the end of our 31-day journey, haven't we? It's been quite a ride, diving deep into faith and rediscovering the true essence of joy right from the core of our being. You feel that too, don't you?

In a month, we have uncovered that joy is a fleeting emotion and a steadfast anchor in our lives. It's an anchor grounded in faith and a close, personal connection with God. During this time, we've realized that joy doesn't shy away from life's challenges but stands firm, reflecting the beauty and growth that stems from our faith in God.

As we wrap this up, I hope this devotional has become a tool, a resource you can revisit, drawing wisdom and joy when needed. And don't hesitate to share the wealth; let others tap into this source of joy we've explored together.

Thank you for being a part of "When Faith Meets Strategy." As you move forward, may your heart be ever aware of the boundless joy God has set aside for you. Carry this joy with you, nurture it, and let it be a beacon of light in your ongoing journey with God.

Counting It All Joy,

Joy,

Founder of When Faith Meets Strategy.